So Far

So Far

Fred Wah

Talonbooks • Vancouver • 1991

Published with assistance from the Canada Council.

Talonbooks
201 - 1019 East Cordova
Vancouver
British Columbia V6A 1M8
Canada

This book was designed by Sally Bryer Mennell, typeset in Novarese
by Pièce de Résistance Ltée., and printed in Canada by Hignell Printing
Ltd.

First printing: September 1991.

Canadian Cataloguing in Publication Data

Wah, Fred, 1939 –
  So Far

  Poems.
  ISBN 0-88922-290-8

  I. Title.
PS8545.A43S6 1991   C811'.54   C91-091490-7
PR9199.3.W32S6 1991

Acknowledgements

Border Crossings, Western Interior, West Coast Line, Beyond Tish, Zest, Writing, Credences, Rootdrinker, Poetry Australia, Span, The Edmonton Bullet, Poetry Canada Review and Chronicle, Somewhere Across the Border, The Malahat Review.

For especially designed classroom editions: Jorge Frascara ("Scree-Sure Dancing"), Peter Bartl ("Exits and Entrances to Rushdie's Sentences"), and Roy Miki ("Dead in My Tracks").

Limestone Lakes Utaniki has been published in a limited edition designed by James Holroyd and in a limited trade edition designed by Peter Bartl for Red Deer College Press.

for Jenefer for Erika so far

Scree-Sure Dancing

home-truths pin-apples part fossil through fertilization flight or
eyesight could be sky or ducks fishing

recognize the plumes   of a Spanish kind of writing
ancestors   as certain types of Atlantic
animals   something from Anatolia   with an ''im'' !

History of the sky engenders the diverse faces of religion
All kinds of stuff like hooks and coat hangers inflate and imprint there

                              Trace
                                   (d)

War on your back
Raw no-words ruin
Real Clear Nuclear

''Ever try to copy Texas?
All those beans, all that plastic?''

— ''I can hardly keep the road plowed.''

HERE WE EVENTUALLY ~~THERE~~ EVEN VELOCITY A TIDE SUN
(SQUINTING) CIPED PAST THE ART THE SURREALISM OREGON
JUST HELP YOURSELF CLEAN UP EGYPT AS A PLACE IN BRAZIL
BUT NO FURTHER EAST TIME AND RICE SEPTEMBER BURNT
TEST TEST

thoughts different
sky's all animals, all
paper, all chalk. Our

writing as		the tableaus
anamorphous	=	of voyage
river cliffs		forgetting

She danced the strict linguistic sense.
babbled bavardage   finger-painted thick
memo-clouds in the darkening sky

$h_{om}{}^{om}e$

That's the secret
              ticket
                    to silence
na (frame) na's notation

. . . each box of art jangles (peut-être)
a purchase on the edge of its own sequence
reflects adjacent body-language events even foreign
the container of *white* we unfortunately call history.

ohh   at nigh   night

Egypt

eh^x_____ap^{i}s_____apex

Maybe it was a dream grammar mountaining out the hypostatic river
as an approximate desire but instead stretched striding or what I
count on under the cedar tree down by the road for final blue prints
to the heart's property.

cellular memory linked to sunset effect
so *sunyata* revealed as absolute closure

I want one ethnic thing here,
right from the start. Dis-
orientation.

January birds
huddle on top of chimney
Wind the letter "A"

Loki, you
stomach

my sound.

Whenever I smell the raiments of message or caprice on you
I get jealous and re-invent old dance asterisks without code*.

*echoes

All the city
song, the great
city air.

What does Qu'Appelle mean?

Did you know I watered the Japanese Cherry out front?

The Manchurian Plum too.

How late did Jenefer sleep on Sunday?

I talked to my mom about using the wormy cherries for wine. Tell her about the worm in the tequila.

What did Erika do at Gray Creek?

I picked two cocoon-like burls off the apricot tree.

What do you think they are?

I think we should plant more flat or sugar peas from now on.

I cooked that halibut with some vegies and the left-over burnt brown rice.

I'm trying to remember a particular and specific rotten two-by-four on the deck or a blemished shingle so I can take us there by mentioning it to you, like that piece that's soft to the touch of my foot when I turn to the left side on "slantingly flying," the one you might feel with your heel as you turn the southwest corner, leaves or weeds in your eyes.

I don't think Peter and Patty will stop here. It's thirty miles north of the transcanada.

You can't swim in the lake here because of the algae.

I don't have a printer for my computer so I'm using a typewriter. There's a girl here who has an old Smith-Corona portable of her mother's which is just like yours only in better shape.

This place is full of noise because it's a band camp and there's a black lab right outside my window howling all night every night.

When I flew over Invermere the fires were really chugging out huge smokestacks so you could tell the mountains were in control.

They have mosquitoes here.

Is life work?

Where is my olive-green tank top?

I don't know if my grandmothers ever talked to one another.

Do you know that idea about if you image something it will be true?

There are probably images in our lives which will never be actualized.

Particularly ones about the north.

Information is definitely not narrative (or maybe narrative isn't narrative).

Could someone (and I don't mean in the Japanese sense at all) clean out the culverts on the road in case there's a real deluge.

Sean's here too.

The food's mediocre.

I'm hoping to go to Regina for Saturday.

I've been fighting a cold.

Tomorrow I'm going to get a ride to town and then walk back. It's 3 miles.

I've discovered when I talk about a poem I'm too "academic." This worries me but maybe it's ok. Like, I don't think it's a serious problem. But if it becomes part of a life-force blowout I'll really wonder.

Don't forget to check the water in the batteries in this hot weather.

What does Qu'Appelle mean?

Hermes Poems

For all that place
hidden behind glass
and silent tortoise-stone shell
rocks for eyes

further
walked footsore for years
just to have a look
snuck up on smouldered night
seen cloaked by day

The harbour's for the ear and the view. Out there a minor fourth foghorn claims large chunks of life. Sun glints off a powerboat windshield. Someone waves between waves, disappears. Boats bob. Risky staring

Victory Square
lots of chairs
for sitting on
outside in

Sillowing of work buzz at the edges, kitchen shadows. Sudden departure. Pecky meandering. Drumming day.

Hermes is a package of crackers

in Ierapatra
a motor bike
a taxi stand
a tour agency
rentacar

broken windmill spokes
solar water heater
man on a donkey

a blue plastic bag
a red plastic bag
a hotel in Rhodos

turkish

Hermes is a snack bar
at the corner of Georgiou Kyrmixali
and Nikolaou Plastira
smoking

a hotel near the Plaka

and he comes from the mouth of an animal
on top of a cement mixer called Heracles

There's a goose sitting on a nest on top of a piling. What at first I
thought was her mate isn't. Turns out to be a loon, further out, bobs,
then looks, pokes its nose into the lake, under. Looks down from
that noonday above. Poke, poke. Beyond all this creative stuff are
the mountains. A trail turns around a large boulder. Subito.

Hrbr

water
scooters
boats fish

eat out
at night
and a light

house har-
bour kalimera
ave maria

hawa
evening
our mothers too

havoc

Men's mothers and the doorway bavardage. Arms folded, hips to
post, toe tapping. This is the shore, the ebb in ebony.

Cretan wheels scribble
push at the walls of the island
night after long night

Translate coop and the desire for a perfect fit. Kaboom. Snap a vector
until some word for steering gets there. Gyproc or wood.

"if one falls and . . ."

jet-skyed
sand-filled
star-specked
girl-drenched
steel-netted
feet-pressed
house-whited
mortar-channeled
sun-paired
sandal-quiet

wrist-brushed
heart-weighted
"rock-hung
chain . . .
broken"

Not this is what you see but this is what you say. You seeing. This
trip a kind of samskara to scare out the europe ghosts. It's as close
as you've come to the old, old world — dead, dead europe. But you
say it simplex, just to yourself. That's no good for these similes, one,
then many. The world needs to be talked to, sung to. Some blind
thing or poet. Some word rivering alongside.

First Pickerel

double bone and all around the fish images of northern
lakes all of them or each one freezing over with latitude
and the double bone comes out of the mouth with a
warning to the tongue and throat then what about the
fish scale skin and human face frozen thereafter or before
in such a fish thinking ahead of the fisherman the catch
and the slip of the tongue to make the hook hold curious
places in taste here such ice water imaging cast up into
the mouth I mean from the driftwood and all that grey
and white breeding

Second Pickerel

imagine the bird as a fish swimming those ducks streaks
eating weeds stuffed skin crisp bone dry also sing about
going straight ahead to China carp or ling cod on the walls
of the water and being there is all it takes for the sky to
feel full of Canada Geese over any watery world now and
Osprey jet blue burst or propelled coloured name after
some other lake you don't know but with fish now think
of those feathers wet smooth and

Third Pickerel

strange to think so much fish on the prairie subject of pleistocene history and sedimentary scalar too K. said Winnipeg was a dish the city an old lake bed then horizon seems more than flat so ocular to look up out of this old water at sky and beach line precision and quietness of the noonday pond solitary vector of fish or insect surface actually bubble-tension again that learning-to-swim horizontal ladder notion not climbing to but through the stars

Fourth Pickerel

Homer you wanderer home again imprinted ocean
through implant by foreknowledge feeling the fluid map
to get to the fighting of the mind against being taken
spelled out clearly to itself the right idea of the right ocean
river or creek to the very gravel fighting the mind against
not getting there home again home again to the heart that
stellar steering of the passage junction box genetic to
contain the image you didn't know any better it wasn't
that she might have been waiting for you home is so
singular nothing else is appropriate to the mind which
carries it so easily hero this is it when you get there and
back again now we know that's why Helen said so

Fifth Pickerel

Gimli's pickerel cheeks for lunch the mountains distant
snow I thought Lake Winnipeg via Gimli Peak in the
Valhallas could be looked at there but here soft tender
pocket or flesh pouched as frozen or upheaved waves
of ice Pauline thought caught in mid-air such leaps under
the surface under the belly get carried away to all those
foreign european countries even until being there later
the snow corn the high hot sun the cheeks flushed

Sixth Pickerel

Walleye at the Bemidji Union voices in the train broiled
he says to do the cheeks in wine or beer but the flounder
w/ shrimp vision of the right brain O Canada a Pike they
call it nothing to match hemispheres in the drive for the
perfect fresh sky looking up out of Digby ''gut'''s right
finding bottom feeder flesh somewhere bluer and cold
glacier line literally has projected into the 10,000 lakes
across a water border invisible except to unseen
electromagnetic rivers running through the starry way
reflected in the lake no wall was

The Water, The Fish

23rd of January after the full moon fish
frozen new year cheeks all day salmon spawn
radio yak yak on the silted creeks
thawing Slocan River and Grohmann's mouth iced all winter long
and there was Nancy from Nemo across the street
know my half-life this year turn-around now to get home
with all of it, the map intact
imprint print

April *or maybe* March

just this chance touching of you each night
this build-up in the bones under sleep's murky plans
this reservoir of unfamiliar language
near you this disturbed tug of body limb
heart-logged this shore or that
this flailing mind behind your tired sighs all that
core, root

all night the assizes of the years
holds this life at revised angles and intervals
this clamour for America's eyes
all around us "small month's meagerness"
every day precious tonguings accent a fever
words float through the dark freer than ever
do you know what I mean, this
feeding at the creek mouth
while we wait for the final coordinates

Getting the Signal Crossed

I'm thinking of Steve and how he'd say all these *things*.

The cool air laps at the open window. Cars drive around

up and down the streets, such beautiful bodies, he'd say.

The world of the soul is lost to the mind. St. Augustine,

it's all your fault. Smoke from the mill indistinct

from the mist grazes along the mountain shoulders (localized

showers in the trees). *Syntax* comes to town this week.

The images don't count t.v. says. To be a woman,

think of a god. (Steve just smiles. He has eyes). South America

comes a little closer. Tiahuanaco fingers the sky with thought.

Tacticless among the trees. Last night this was called

"Getting the Signal Crossed." Notes on history

to play with. Music — you don't know when it's going to stop.

Call it "Sammy the Salmon" and come home.

What Prevails

the trees this morning and the clouds
today the same old mist-hackled mounts argue
the stability of the unchanging present
every day my mind drives up the road along the lakeshore
valleys of unavoidable distances on the shoulder
when what prevails isn't rhythm
but the poet's death
(they think)
on the eve of a new fascism
the kokanee have forgotten the way home
the spawning channels will be there long after
the rust Todorov says Poetry protects us from
even that line a trace of old track
whole geographies, continents, pass by
there's a light February snow today
and a loop in the sememe
that lets me dance.

The Stairs
to Bob and Smaro on the Star River

I always thought of stars on your stairs too.
Rising from that prairie "dish" up to thought, thinking
and the talk talking huge night sky
always something like the "emic" displacement
hovers in the rush of frozen air through the door
(how smart the builders are
to place it at the foot of the stairs
like a decompression chamber, up
and up literal to vertical possibility in your two minds
your voices unmeshed and scattered by desire.

I'll tell you, the stairs are perfect,
still used for each step of the return.

Accidents of Colour 1

Everyone I know here
gets dressed up for winter
dreaming

so much brown, pink, so
much cold
Mary's scarf, little fur toque

red coat boat white
"writing my seeing"
riding my sea out

Accidents of Colour 2

Colour my hat
McNaughton

the blue blue sky here on the prairie
you chose or was it
the yellow nearly mustard wool

stripes knit, horizon
plus the sun too and the frozen land
bright in a short day

such spaces, deserts, wasted words
I look at my watch and walk

you decide.

Accidents of Colour 3

Pam your pretty red boots
orange beaded feet blue
mind signed to thinking body connected
strung to the storm outside
the letter *e* floats
(electronique)
in the dish, on the horizon
through the snow

albescent on the South Saskatchewan overbody
all air and larger, grasses and smaller
if you face north it changes
                              cutbank
                         into the mind
unexpected brown twists, nothing to stop the eye
therefore nothing there outside nothing
or just a little pink
                         (yesterday when it rained
everything

Winter Day

We expect more snow today and the birds will have to put up with it and so will all small things. Trees' limbs outlined by the snow they carry. All the dark things in winter. In the cow pasture behind our house the apple trees are frozen stiff and underneath the snow the first frost has been driven into the dirt. This large quietness, even with the train whistle in the valley, is the soft underbelly of the snow-clouds settled in the mountain trenches, caught in the trees, against the rock faces, electric lines hum the warmth between our minds and our places.

Alpine

the small grass
clings to the alpine scree
seed-head heavy
breeze-frozen
rock

•

we want some of that autumn orange
that yellow, and that, and that
and give us more
of that dead red too

•

two days after we picked our dead mountain bouquet
I have thought three times at least of the wave sounds on some beach
and now the cello and shakuhachi
low roar of the wind up the slopes

•

the transparent and the brittle
this is all I do as I touch them
they break
bald anemone, dry
arnica seed
paper-clean

Blue Grouse Basin
for Wendy Hurst

I knew when I came down the trail
and saw the shine in your eyes going up
all words for this day were yours.

frost-nipped huckleberries
sorrel maybe by the mine shaft
Fennel (I believe in the colour of maps
more than anything else)
snapshot of toe-baby and fireweed
alone now in this first snow meadow
water so pure, Plato
would have changed his mind

Spring Geography

Things appear suddenly
not new but as they remain
left over from the winter

for example, dead logs
caught in the brush at all angles
a breathing pushes out from them

a picture in the warmer air
sings out
to the surfaces of our skin and eyes

a handfull of dead fingernails
I love you today
like I have never before

fingers and hair, dead logs
heads hands twigs sticks
leaves grass the suddenness

and warm air shimmering
off the hood of a green
'47 Dodge pickup

mountains
come out of the clouds
the road down
to the lake

Sorrel Leaves
for Nancy Jean

got those sorrel leaves in mouth
taste of rock sand as root deep down
underneath as mineral water brought to leaf
large glass mirrors that cast argenta taste
remembering a place east of yourself
                                        (old lakes)
the memory of view strata layer
to register glacial rivers milk as sorrel outwash
green leaf sediment eyes horizon mount
saint helen's hair and taste of years

Writing the Translating
for Jenefer

west arm boats all time drift moving and saying left-over
Jenefer you'd know this view maybe from your north or
what remains of a blond genetic flow your body getting
back up from the fall the ocean of embarrassment you
can remember floating up from the ice into the heat of
July now thawed to a greener place so that what remains
is more than this lake which is likewise fed by water from
somewhere else in turn no mistake a further shore of
incompleted driftwood.

Building Poem

Try to get to sleep
build headers and roof pitches
make up the construct
windows, doors
snow sliding off into the abyss
what more can we do inside
build otherwise, renovate
make things just right

as expected
fix everything that breaks
store the wood
the chainsaw the snowblower the tools
the tools all over the place
everything hidden and lost
never know
the woodpile falls far away into the falling snow
what matters when you and I build at night
as sleep takes on the actual plan

the mind's plain or landscape
go out and snap a line
is there enough room
twenty feet by the width
height plum
to the tops of the trees sky
where will the stove be
will the sun hit its south wall
where will the rain run to

so on down
sleep comes
in the imagination of the building
eyes shut over angles snowloads footings and beams
instead of seducing you or travelling to the bifrost

Her House

Her mind and life-
time, yearning

for her life's
mind on it, heart

dance, literally
with her mouth

shoulders too
today years ago

I married her.
Outside, the distant glaciers

crack and groan
with the same desire.

Opening Up To You

opening up to you,
                    baby
I thought we'd dance across the floor
always try to keep available they say
those others
the ones with perfume in the Massachusetts air
behind them

I say let's go
and then I can't
but you, you're gone
on a sea of smell
puffed out in front of yourself
spinnaker
making for the new world

Translating Translating Appollinaire
vis-a-vis bp

SOLEIL
        the sun rolls off my back

cou

coupé
        the snow falls into the world

cold

        put yr boots on an yr toque
        wax wing's brittle

older
      into the world a little

leaf   from the sky

sky
      from the sky

Anthropomorphia

                        stickle ceiling
rain (that's the forecast)
       joy

                  how do I know this will work

can't stop it
       to the world

                    the hildergast

pole

            connected if you're a mouse
river if you're a fish
                morphia
                        falling

          to the east
in the west

              death's stick the tool

       same thing
the symmetry of accident spills again
hands reach out to help, there's a Shell station on the right
bullrushes line the ditches, fenceposts line the land
the hydro lines
               get nowhere
     joy stops
a rainbow settles it for the sky

Picket Line

on the picket line
we could dance like a bird
old magpie, woodpecker
raven the thief
caw and peck
wiggle and get sassy
speak the spike
strut the truth

words are really gut smart

make it look the way you want
that's what images are wanted for
at the end

music is like that too, you know
exactly when
and what's next in song

and then right in the ear
sounds get together in cognizance
how

can you do it,
the words don't come from other worlds
each is a time sign

remembers itself only once
between all other words

far away

flowers that I didn't know
and rivers
      (the mountains, everything you can hold
      you sit in, not

this spectacle of the silent life
and the desire which goes on without you, words
flow too
      (the tree is a part
      so simple it stands
      and blossoms and blossoms

you needed to know the events
like light and food
where to go next
and you didn't
      (I'm thinking a flower a river a flower
      new sights of the new to remind mind

this pensive, this light idea
with the body, this
life of its own
      (the narrative symbiosis, bark-cork
      to beach
      wood
        sand
      Williams' "lips"

all this movement away from one another is unnecessary
it could be Mexico City

thinking thinking outside the landslide
lying of the tongue, outright
lies of the trees — a little
wind and light snow to tell the truth
at the foot of the glacier
the water laps the shore.

The Bird Part Of It

Oar sticks in the lake. Moon and stars colourless.
This bird will get to be a part of it, you between.

China makes noise. When my mother read Pearl Buck.
Let's see — Pearl, Yellow, and there's that other one.

Grain of the sun which is the key to your thighs.
Luce meles I mean. Skilled as a rower, a waver.

Not for sport. Sail, sunset, etcetera.
Oarswoman, Tisserande, and the crows.

Stars are like that. Shove it.
Stillness is everywhere tonight. Pierceless rocks.

We say admiringly how the loon oars the water.
Heaven is simple. A river. My horn of.

Stars are genetic. Salt.
After all, those wounds are for her. Thus music, too.

Stone-meal, sin, plenty of it, That's advertising.
My little woman of the night. In Japan, it's true.

Puts or pushes or sticks or shoves his always.
-euse, euse.

Maybe my Grandmothers went North
(after David McFadden)

Here I am on the prairies again listening to a voice
telling me I should be further north. But I'm not
ready. There's no one else with me. The grass has been eaten
by grasshoppers or is all dried up. Every person I have known
in this landscape has moved to another town, but none of them
have gone any further north.

Neither of my grandmothers
learned to drive. I don't know if they ever had mushrooms
to cook with. It was pretty dry here then too. They hardly ever
smiled but when they did they were indoors. Maybe
the earth heaved with ecstasy, maybe not.

The Poem Called Syntax

We live on the edge of a lake called Echo.
I love this notion that noise makes itself,
so the lake holds all noise in its depths
and when the dog barks it gets it from the lake.

About nine thousand feet above these lakes (all lakes)
there is a geometry of sound, something like Plato's cave of noise.
It is from that construct the dog's bark takes shape,
a resounding of an earlier bark conditioned by the alpine.

History and physics. Acoustic paradigms in a bog of algae.
When I tell all my cousins and friends about this
they'll come to live on the shores of this lake and clean it up.
From the balconies of their summer homes they'll ask a lot of
    questions.

two bears from nowhere, at least
the mind brought back

fog in the valley
life, the hands tell

horse made of trees
a labyrinth of space and time silent

the bears quiet now
maybe the horse whinnies

just for a moment you don't want to know
too much

the bottoms of the trees become huge roots
gnarled, really, this moment past being

Weather

Where I live
when I wake up in the morning's dark
I listen for the plow down on the road
to find out
if it snowed overnight
or not to the
soft
snow's
silence
plow's
scraping, distance
distant
in the valley

A Snow Poem for Pamella

I saw your eyes in the lift-line today
crisp, just below freezing, words
caught in the treetops
blue sky and the hoar-frost line lifting to an incoming fog
there's more
later you're a mother breastfeeding in the lodge
the hill very white
and your eyes looking through the winter air
all over me these words
with only your smile
eternal events

Javanese music to the end
call for Duncan in Damascus
sounds like bells are like bells
the lines to the street
leave his stairway to the eye
onlooker
around the world travel
sounds like size/picture
the news *ta'wil* method serious
music soft and thinks about it
other places sounds minds
you and Dan in the ancient city

March Music

Sounds roll beautifully from the piano. A precious accent lines the air on this mountainside. The contemporary earth comes again, again sings, self-seeking, circumstantial, but with a drum, a drum: full dominant seventh rolled out on the white snow still left in the cow pasture of a mirror, ayee, all the work of the skin, thaw coming up through the gravel road, truth rests, that's right, in memory, symmetric and outside the silent, not so simple as the dogs barking at the shadows in the tree-line, Thursday, think of the thunder ahead.

Almost
for Erika

Almost don't dare look at the sky these nights for the
largest moon of the year October tells and a full red sky
in the West too down to the rivers below Mount Sentinel
huffing it such seasons this valley from our walk along
the back road up past McDougal's tonight and the dogs
dogs more bite in the air than memory all of a sudden
we come up our road under the cedar tree Erika I know
that's yours and your mom's moon again how make it
imagic words to tell you I love you and here, here's some
of this hillside of your heart's such a large large sky.

Birthday Poem
for Erika

the dog said woof woof real low like he was talking to
you he said let's go I'll follow you or grohw grohw far
back in his throat watch out out there now the dog is a
log on the beach floating in our dreams he appears when
you need to cross water or brush your teeth in this world
we take our dog everywhere we go even over mountain
passes in early October just to remember each year
lapping lapping the same sure shore

Permanent Spirit

the "permanent spirit" turns
pages, the lexicon turns to
numbers, names, and the vague outlines of names

(bare birch of November) nothing
remains after the words
wet leaves

cold substrate of the precessions
motions of the stars
the tongue literally sings through those signs

(buzz)-frost without the body
unable to unscatter the scatter
tremendous volume of light

this is their white bark which coheres
to each phrase, the rest soil
mountain, root-rock

clean tatters shed the mouth
book of the forest uncut hillsides
self-interviewed gutter what fork, sweep

I get up in the morning
and the cloudy skies are in my legs.

The news at the door lies
under the guise of someone else's pulp mill.

In the shower I smell creosote,
my brain drinks up the pressure-treated ions.

You choreospect around the kitchen all egg,
you say my eyes have dreamed nothing.

Your eyes. Mine squint from the winter sun,
they read about the world, foothills in the distance.

They read languageless heads subtract
language. No more poems until.

Each day depletes a little more mith (sic),
mouth logged — logos scaled and decked.

Her tall body twirls, bone-rippled ankles lift.
We could count, we could dance that way.

outside up
the hill
Blackie's full
load of
hemlock spruce couple
sticks of cedar Meadow
Mt. to Lardeau six
teen minutes eleven
seconds re
carbo
nation

How to Get Across the River
Any River

Drive northeast to a point on the old road
where you join a cortex of scars left by loggers.

After the container stop and look north
below the ridge the mouths of two small caves.

The veins are filled with words, stories really,
and the further away they extend, the more striated.

Just our luck to live here on this side of the valley
on a hill with a perfect view

and a garden. Has the gutter on this
page, this old paper bridge, washed out

yet?

This is about Chile

The credit bureau phoned for his address today
but I told them I've lost touch.

Him asking me, then me talking you, Winnipeg and Nelson
diagrammatically arising from the dry horizon.

Why don't you right now try hard to be
about Chile?

Have a cup of coffee, sit in the morning air
look at what they do, pucker your eyes and ears

Say *Siempre.*
But it's only biology.

Come back to the numbers.
Pay your phone bill.

Cow Poem

Sticky with frost
Sleeping with fire

I am a cow
Caught in a storm

My eyes open
Legs arthritic

Heartsore from dream
My mouth nailed shut

I can smell smoke
The snow is dry

On my shoulders
Gate of apples

Open ridgepole
Sky of grey words

Numbers as trees
Thick solitude

We don't get it
Such a long ride

Is this ocean
On the level

Limestone Lakes Utaniki

Saturday, August 1/87
I talk to myself this morning, on the long drive up the Columbia valley. I notice that, that I talk to myself more than to others, I say that to myself, that and where we're going, the fresh of the morning, the truck packed with hiking gear, that, and that. Pauline and I meet the others at the Skookumchuk Cafe for the long drive up the gravel logging road valleys, people eyes ahead faces set on the next step, a chopper lift up to 8,000 ft. in the Rockies east of Invermere. But the weather socks in during the day so after I wrap the truck in chickenwire, mezmerize alone, lean on a log long hours but no chopper, unwrap the car and spend the night there, strewn w/ cloud (I hope stars).

This afternoon I unzipped the pocket of my pack and found this journal, left or lost since last summer's hiking camp in Anemone Pass in the northern Selkirks. In it I find this poem I wrote in response to Pat Lifely's fall from a cliff during the first days of the camp.

A *Garnet for Pat Lifely*

Here's a small encrusted stone for your cairn,
home for you.

this wine-red nipple of the January mind
your death fell from
every day we face them
those rock bluffs across the valley, a pine,

large alpine sky arches over these slopes each night
oh wonder of rock and water and earth

what alchemical lake we and this are

This then
periodic counting
not-forgotten alpine meadow winter sod
under all this weight of place:

wind too
flowers we've named, snow
patches, ledges, creeks, lakes, marmots, eagles, clouds

and on to the face we glass each day
that bluff between our eyes
lake and the waterfall
                                        striations
of a life
                            simple single
gouge in rock

Hah!
        have you become our pet cow-bird
        hop for mosquitoes at meal time?

        is that you, then, already disappeared further south
        w/ the cariboo?

This garnet, such a little thing to leave here for you.

But birds have that quick and darting look — they know
winter's coming,
                    that
they don't decide.

The stones of paradise ripen. We pick them up as reminders,
touchstones, like the clock of the Big Dipper, filligree of mind
set on never sinking below the horizon, or in migration as a
way home.

The best ones are found close to treeline or snowline or
browline. Sometimes the line is recognized after the rock's been
pocketed, but only with distance.

Lines can be cracks, as in an avalanche.

Sunday
   This morning we still wait for the first sound of the chopper in the clouds. Gusty and raining a bit. All day I either sit in the car and work with the words, talk to myself, or walk along the gravel road alone and taste the old work, summer timber cruising.

               Years ago nothing in the sky
               gray whales of cumulus floated slow all day
               at the head of the valley

               just another gravel road
                        w/ clear-cut rubble down to the creek

               Late afternoon over the washboard
               pickup truck a trail of dust

               or a wet October Sunday
                        —all the gravel roads so settled down, quiet
                                all alone

   Finally, in the late afternoon, the cloud ceiling lifts a bit and the chopper comes through. He gets us in before supper. Tents set up on a small pond-filled bench and we start to feel the spread of place, dewed grass, boots, flashlights, bite of air in the nose.

   Gravel, garnet, granite, seed, tree, mountain — all ones also inescapably in Thoreau's choice of the Milky Way just like every logging road I come across I run over the stardust again until the soul sings *Oh!* or even talking to myself the same old rhythm, breathing but with notice of the weather, the time of day even.

67

Monday

From the camp we hike up about 1,000 ft. We'll have to do this most days to reach the range of rambling available. I walk along a stunning grey and red limestone highway/arena, huge typochronic wave-swirl of razor rock. Patches of cliff-clinging grass and flowers. Pauline can't understand why I don't get into the names, like "something poisonous something" (Elegant Poisonous Camus) or Fringe Grass of Parnassus. So as I walk along talking that one out to myself I figure that naming is more than only counting, that it also works for me as a very particular image, like Nancy-Jean's "sorrel" up Kokanee, or I'm always looking for saxifrage on the edge of my eye, that one lonely flower (maybe "mist maiden" or "mountain aben") she called me back up the scree to photograph in Anemone Pass last summer. Yet there is that surface of experience, say, just walking and breathing, eg. tables of limestone today with little islands of schist sticking up into the vibram almost like velcro. But the problem with naming is number, you can't look at, let alone count, all of it.

Like right now after lunch someone yaps "get the maps" and I think of the maps folded up in my pack and how I never really use them for the specific, just an overview (imaginary mostly).

How easily lost
I could get

Back in camp I play around with a watercolour card for Liz, the young teenager who hiked with us today.

The goat.
She thought.
She saw.

68

I think we acquire surfaces of a world and that's what becomes the planar echo or projection called flowering which later could be the ghost-like residue of skin, leaf, or story and other filmed shapes of ceremonial intimacy.

Tuesday
I've spent all day chasing after but never finding the people I started hiking with. They were going around a ridge I hiked up over and I lost them. Everywhere I look — no trace. Disappeared. I've scrambled up a couple of high hills, yelled, yodelled, scanned, and listened to my nervous breath. Now I've sort of given up, had a bath in the ice-cold lakes.

Not lost
Heart beats
Alone
All day
Long
Day all
Alone
Beats heart
Lost not.

To not shout loud enough into the pond is ok, it'll still be there next penetrating some veiled alliance, rephrased portrait, reverse scheme stuck in the throat we depend on to cut into place when needed, hopeless levers of cyclicity sentencing device to sameness so as to clip the cry at the stomach-carving thrust over the lakes and across the valley, still here, mouthing out the cave.

Wednesday

Fingers stiff and cold as I write this because a wet front moved through last night. Mist hackles hang and float so I decide to stay in camp for a few hours and fiddle around with a pin-hole camera. Pauline, Liz, and I amble off later on to Waterfall Lake just above us and then to Limestone Lakes where I photo and paint for an hour.

A picture of shooting-star that primrose easy day connections in my body brush chromatic hills and mountains dilute gray those pigments glinted out the corner of cerulean blue above (no black or white) but Winsor green dark burnt umber raw sienna cadmium yellow watered yellow ochre for the lakes the limestone hills and wet blue paper for the sky left o.

Nothing's wrong here. This is the palace This is the place.

Thursday

Today Pauline and I hike off alone down to Sylvan Pass roundabout but we overshoot height and there we are on a ridge above the pass so the day is really a trial until I realize on the way home we discover foot ramps of rock and grass down to and up from each wee lake and that sidehilling elk cut across to the ridge before Longview Peak gets us sheer height above what down below five foreign backpackers cut across the gray and red amphitheatre. From there we make plans for home. Down on the limestone floor we sit on the lip of a huge sinkhole river rumbling hundreds of feet beneath and after that the trip back's a maze of diagonals along the arcades finally down to a lake to swim and bathe and by mistake find our way out again.

Ancient ochre valley
hosts rock events
but the elk find human trails around everything.

Trust those trails
and we won't get any more lost
than all of us already are.

Subterranean river tracking the needed code recognizes tulle
of ocean/desert reflective saying animal palm's line earth outer
voice radioed position echoing in on carbon some seed still
packed with palace so salmoning home.

Friday
Last day of camp so I think to amble off alone to get some height
above the west lakes. I get up on a ridge above the milky glacial
lake, perfect blue summer sky today. But then I get hooked into or
onto what looks like an easy ridge to make. I keep climbing and each
next ridge seems an ok way up. Gradually it becomes a cling, the
rotten rock leans out and back. Near the top I have some difficulty
in a chimney and remember that time long ago in the Lardeau when
I couldn't go down and couldn't go back up. When I finally reach
the summit it's mostly a worry about getting back down — too much
adrenalin to eat lunch. But a different chute opens up to me on the
way back down and delivers me onto a safe-enough ledge where
I breathe little sigh at last.

So fear alone pummels itself inward to itself
and becomes a fossil of another life

a piece of elk shit that lives siliconed rock hard under
geomorphic seabeds

a limestone sinkhole in the dark caverns of our falling
stomachs

an unnameable saxifrage that cracks and breaks the rock
    face

the little avalanche of boulders that crackle out onto
    sheets of muddy ice and snow

the rotten Rockies rock that crumbles in the middle of
    a footstep or handhold

red-algaed snow-patch too steep and icy to use

razor edge of ice and the hidden gap under the feet

this black schist or flint in the gray limestone

that's where that fear is

held there for you

alone

alive.

Uluṟu Utaniki

to Jenefer

Friday, July 28/90
Today is Jenefer's birthday tomorrow on the other side of the date line. The plate tectonics fold ocean's time lap here, shore to shore — she'll be driving into the heat, away from the coast, through the Okanagan desert and into the mountains and into old umbilical remnant Kootenay Lake. Time. For a dip.

> Low roar of sea-surf shakuhachi under
> echo

> Dull thud of chi-stone
> cool in the macrowave

> white noise and no coral underbrush
> resonant hint in synch but wide

We walk clockwise around Ayer's Rock this morning. The trail is quiet, clear of the crowds who ant up and down to the top. North now. We pass Kantju Gorge, full of a tour bus-full hurrying in and out, leave it alone.

> A little chill in the lee
> sun edged shadow slit strung

> her walk is all her own bones
> held

> Love O distant love
> winter gum leaves pacific in the sand

Inside stooped under torped overhang we scan the paintings overhead. This is a gate to place. Stop. The paint travels direct dot act. Swirl of salt wash turbined rock moves into farther implants. We are in our walking shoes today.

There's that white leaf
Mala Puta pouch of the female hare-wallaby

how earth sits
those fellas sit

silt of the river stilled stories posed
reposed

Just before we come around the corner into the sun there's a women's
sacred site fenced off. Silence and the sacred. Secret. East now and
a bit of breeze. Male site escarped on corner base.

Pocked mouth shut
door to the Wilytja (house) shut

Park ranger signpost words
the line of knowing on the face

far-looking rock in desinence
d-sign polarized to Cancer?

The north-west corner of the rock is a cleft slit through sandstone
sun-glint henge-like horologe. We've seen the score from the start
and it leads us — led with the eye through light. Unseeable distance.
Blind. Aperture. Daytime night blade.

Gap to blink bridge
Gondwanaland

or the eye of silent estimation
makes another meso-connection

kidney carried
pearl stone

Such a screen of silence on the face of the rock. The stories are there,
that's obvious, but they aren't telling. A light wind as we come into
the sun. A quiet wind. A fence keeps us distant from the large sacred
site of fallen boulders along the north edge.

Tongue-tied track of memory
red-etched glyph

typos scarred with old info
can't decrypt these chips of the "hole" story

— now to architect the dream eme
take rope, take water.

We finally work through the trees and awesome mountain images
above to Muṯiṯjulu, the one story, home of Wanampi the water snake.
Here Kuniya ritually drops sand to help control the forces of anger.
There are the spears.

Dogma of extension focusses on the outskirts
nomadology hums to itself (walking along)

silence
always a field of secret legwork

mindfullness dances the polarity, measure
no number

Dead in My Tracks: Wildcat Creek Utaniki

Saturday, July 29/89
Oh golden, Golden morning!

   West of Golden we leave the trans-Canada and drive north about 60 k up Blaeberry River past Doubt Hill. From the chopper site we can see south to Howes Pass, a long sweep of valley brilliant in a pillowed mid-summer heat-haze. An hour's spent wrapping the cars and trucks in chicken wire (old paranoid alpine parking-lot visions of the imaginary porker chewing our tires and rad hoses). Camp's just west, a ten-minute bezier curve, swirl, and plop up Wildcat Creek, on a west slope facing east to the contintental divide ridgeline of the B.C./Alberta boundary.
   Ringed by glaciers as usual
   Ayesha, Baker, Parapet.
   While we set up camp during the afternoon I'm in a global mode, you know, the simultaneity of the world going on right now. Paris. Kyoto. Beijing. The pavement of Tiananmen Square, the hotlines sniffing out the dissidents, CBC bulletin even e-mail media drama of the last two months still in the air, even up here, radioless, only antennaed in my bones (our name is bones, and your name is my name).

                My Borders are Altitude

            and silent

                              a pawprint's cosine
            climate   from the lake to the treeline
                    all crumbly under foot at the edges
                      cruddy summer snow melt
              soft wet twig and bough-sprung alpine fir
                                            but more than this
            height
                    is my pepper

(China
          don't)
                    Now
(broken breaths contour intervals at the next 100 feet and then
the sky-remembered night on the plateau above the
Saskatchewan Qu'Appelle oh stars what solitude your blue line
and flight or weight the inverse holds me shoulder-to-shoulder
my clouds as alpine meadows Newton would have cut yet
minds find bandwidth in this topos-parabola chaos around the
earth house
          Here's this
               stone under heathered turf
          back bent as I dig and ruffle   sacrum
               drawn to the music
                         a slow and daily pelvic tilt of elevation
     is this numbered boundary nowhere, I'm
     close to 7000 here, maybe I'll just do the horse
                    not to hold the world
                              just touch, complete
                    the circuit
               borders such thin thoughts (apples of our eyes)
                         selvage yesterday's Tiananmen
               a power-line buzz above, along my spine, my legs
     go up and down
                         heart all summer-heavy
                              with the people

Sunday, July 30
   We hike east across the valley toward Mistaya Mountain, as far as
a scree slope on the south side of a grano-diorite carbuncle so
massive we're left only to pick and chip below the heel of.
   Each rock vectors through the eyes to the height of the stomach
and stops me, dazzles, dead in my tracks. Such singular surfaces are
impossible to avoid. Eyes tumble click, stop and stare, stop, stare
at pink molten sunset rivers of limestone, sawtooth schist embedded.
   But at this rate the hike's all history, pleistocene.

No animals, no print, no scat. (Goat tracks? Too faint now to be sure.)
No sky-mirrored glacial swimming holes today.
No fresh water. Heather very dry. The bees buzz. Butterflies.
Doze in the sun at the bottom of a scree slope waiting for the others.

    sugar of their struggle death
    in China's humid night so far away
    maybe that's the simplest equation
    for the headwaters
    television's human river
    and now the sun decreases
    the friction. The fingers
    of my right hand trace
    a band of quartz. My eyes sink
    under the brim
    far away
    but not so far away.

Monday, the 31st
Today we climb the same side of the valley as yesterday. But now
we've taken a keep-more-to-the-left route to a neck or col between
Alberta and B.C., under Mistaya. Lunch beside a snowpatch lake.

    when deconstruing rock
    hold back the crude and the harsh
    or take "reality" for simple target
    the sun
            a nation as large as China
    is just another scheme for thirst and war
    another centered project tunneling earth
        (my father's fingers poked wet into the mud of
        a rice paddy

rumours, the same large-spun sky here
in the thin air and during the long winter
quartz grows with the sparkle of a bridge
every stone on this mountain clicks
some old biotic tumbler locked
unlocked sadness
    not of the hundred-blossomed mountain
    not of the nine-millenia incense
    but of the dragon-slit tongue silenced
    youth before old age

After-lunch drowsiness sets in under the warmth of the sun; no birds sing; not so far away the glacier rivers roar in the July heat.

shale shard weep shard shale weep shale weep shard shale
weep shale weep shard shard weep shale shard weep shale
weep weep shhh

Those rocks this morning on the way up appeared full of signs and messages. So I walked around in a meander and kind of grilled each striated spot for information, news of the conglomerate earth.
       or
           ee
                 ent
The others' words around me buzz and fall like horseflies.
Alberta looks busy from this side; Jasper/Banff another of those new equations to satisfy war's glacial thirst. Ice-blue sky-line jet-tracked.
        ent
            re. Pren
              eur. Prende

The wooden handle of an ice axe stuck in the snow: "When making an ax handle," the pattern is occasionally too far off. Somewhere else. Out of sight, *man*. Out of mind.

snow pond fed by two large drifts vectored off of   morraine.
no real fish.
the Beijing hotline surfaces as jet track reminder
through the high blue air
then sinks at news of the killings.
deep, like a floating thermostat.
deep, like a disappearing hook.
baited.

Tuesday, August 1

I didn't sleep very well last night because I had to get up as breakfast helper this morning — fretted about the alarm on my wristwatch being loud enough and so now mid-afternoon, sit on a slope above what the camp's come to call "crystal gardens" on the cool (windy) side of a grassy knoll tired and lulled by the rush of waterfall across the valley and above this alleyway that led us here full of crystals dangled and hidden for years we poke under little rock ledges.

Quiet here. Light breeze to keep the horseflies down. I glass across a valley to a slope, for yesterday's tracks, but they've melted out. Pan back to a blurry knoll of purple yellow red pink and white on green with songs (I Don't want a Sickle) I can't get out of my head and there're the others, after-lunch sprawl on the heather, Pauline reading in her flower book.

smoke in the wind, the forest below
porcupine under the wire quietly chewing our tires
is that it
smoke in the city,
    slow sweep sweep of a broom in the square

Small thunderstorm coming around Trapper Peak should force us down the hill, while on this beared-over gopher-searching mountainside I linger, stopped, can't keep my eyes off the rocks and surfaces surging to not so much arrest myself in all this "otherness" as greedily scour the dripping quartz for crystal jewels for my daughters. Something lucky, something old. Something eight-spot rooted in rock, fatherness ancestral distance cut.

Hand-held Pictostone

from above Wildcat rockscape of old Renaissance bullet hole or navel with tracks going out the sides a type of Malthusian linear function along the aisles of a Saturday afternoon matinee forever pocked with edge and gouged embedded pebble from distant beach a cracked and weathered map of textured tilt propellor hummed out from omphalic sedimentary lint enough to tell story's history warped high enough in the diurnal headlines from Beijing and Shanghai so that a geologist imagining fake fish in a fake lake scrapes around the edges for shrapnel but me I think in my own mittened photos of the life look out of and far away from these threads through the hole to continue the prospect beyond impact of landing very hard and fast and past the anima button.

New moon tonight.

Wednesday
  A wet day. Drizzle started last night after days of heat. The snow-line is about 8500 feet this morning. Very cool all day, off and on rain and sleet, some hail. And no respite tonight so now I sit/lie in our tent at 9 p.m. still light enough to write. I've put on my toque and gloves. No thought. Just body.

A few of us walked up the valley on the other side of Wildcat Creek and crossed many feeder creeks and the glacier river at the head of the valley. I had to take off my pants and boots once. The water came up to just above the knees. Memoried on and off all day crossing Toby morraine years ago with my brother and Loki and how that crossing, just below the crotch, rejuvenated bruised ligaments. This time my feet remain ice all day.

All these rocks. Constant mirror and prescence in my eyes. More rocks than grains of sand in the whole world, I bet someone. Intricate pattern, surface, keeps stopping boot in pitch for eye to zoom. Sometimes I stop and try translating the imago-grammatic surfaces. What do I look for? This I-Chinging the earth for some other Gate of Heavenly Peace, monotoned loudspeaker in the Square signalling "Go home and save your life," old, embedded said-again family bone-names?

       Scale of shale
       jamb stone, lintel, henge.

       When the door's open
       there's nothing to catch the eye.

       Except the sun (blink). Now this tent
       on the outside of a non-scaled phenomenon.

       We'll see, Fred says to himself, the tree
       as much a cinnabar flag as

       — the mountains folded and folded.
       "with uncountable broken arms and legs floating . . ."

       This sky of clouds, new grass, melon
       summer fields creased .

       By forcing them into the centre of the square
       the indelible occupies the heart until next time.

These "basins of attraction"
these grains, these fractal editions.

Night swoops very low
just a reminder.

Thursday, August 3/89

This morning I sit in the tent writing and try to situate the play in this place. The world today feels all stage. Nothing moves. A set set. There are the huge mist hackles clinging to the mountains, but no history.

Far, far down the valley a chainsaw whines.
At night now some of the creeks disappear.
Winter.

Friday, August 4/89

This last day we hike up to the col between Peto and Mistaya but get caught in a cold mist/fog. Just behind the gauze the oval of the sun teases. The cover didn't break so we don't go further than the snow field. We spend the rest of the day circumnavigating the head of the valley and several glacial lips up and down and home and that's eight and a half hours to a spaghetti dinner and the sky lifting to a blue evening.

Now nearly 9 o'clock and the mosquitoes, after days of rain, are up for it.

Out of the corner of my eye more rocks. And out an ear I hear a few birds sing their particular song, not solitary: the creeks rush and gurgle down to the valley below. In a corner of my mind is tomorrow's two-and-a-half-hour hike out to the trailhead and then the long drive home. But nowhere else.

clear stingin' peaks
                          rock green moss
                                          campion
                    all surface news
                                      inked
to the bloated stone heroes
                        massed alongside Mao's mausoleum
same shards here
                          within the square
                                    a "percolation
                    network"
five lines,
                  five soldiers a line
                                    duende stone
thano-stone

P *You So*

too fast fifty years you're still waiting to dance
antics of old migrations cut through your glance
I want to be with you under every tree
in the hills you hurtle smiles and tongues
scree vectors your legs, stride as you move
miles and miles the rice waits simmered
a little polka in your eyes this tilt of your shoulder
hands counter the air you ride so high o
five o five o content's continent so
wanna dance

Five Ones for P.

Watch you
and then keep
watching you.

More the body, everything
you've touched
tongue and shoulder,
shoulders
dancing too.

I keep watching
you out there, star
you sail, your sky, your moon
all night long almost
shore to shore.

When I'm out there with you
only to be with you,
why else
you're what I know, see you
always have to.

The Bears

All the trees around here are full of bears. Tonight
there is a full moon crying. Friends are upside down.
Animals are trying to think about life for a change.

In the hard light of the spruce trees dusk invites the geese.
Sometimes twice a year the cut-throat trout find the horizon,
the one that sits at the far end of the lake. Children.

Listen, to the cages being rattled. Look in their eyes
and look underneath the cedar boughs. All of us,
no matter how hard it is, plan trips to the prairie.

White Lake

The clouds
and the sun over the Pacific
mistakes about the atmosphere
and voices. And the "Gulf"'s connection
with this woman's frame, Dona (?)
Malinche, Cortez's golden sun
except this is a Pacific cloud bank
(not interested in the thing itself) Flying over White Lake
these hills, lines and lakes the soft snow folds
even coyote in the valley forgets,
even the sparse pine on worn ridges, soft,
soft, even this sprinkle, this edge,
this cold and frozen grass
between our toes.

In the mail with your letter is a package of coupons
for Tom Wayman

minus thirty and they have to deliver this:
order this unbreakable coffee server now
never walk around again
a golden opportunity
forbidden fruit, to go
recoltez 18 cents de Croc-en-ble
solid brass
there is only one
personalized gifts
made a little softer on your pocket
world's first $100
take strokes
keep your car or boat
free
scarios, the new lunchtime treat
your little monsters will gobble up
free career
how much do you know
introduce your family to our family
a personal message from Jean Philippe-LaFrance
economisez
wrap yourself in satin
30 cents de rabais
off
win a beautiful day
slice yourself in
get cracking
tastes fresher than fresh
try another variety
if you love
bet your kids . . . and we're not bluffing
on light-flow days
send for the new

Exits and Entrances to Rushdie's Sentence(s)

ONE. What if the phemic blasted page so what was once transparent appeared an eye-spot burning paper you know with the sun and a magnifying glass erasing words instead of antheming another spiritual mirage imaged fate as predictable as a butterfly's flight plan.

TWO. A scent of the fall sheer memory snow smells meltdown this Everest morph more aperiodic than withershins and less likely resentment unioned by belief as a series of words than in the middle of juncture not standing like dawn hammers over the Himalayas but a flap-and-squawk v-line of geese.

THREE. If you could acquire a migrant invisibility in exchange for, say, sixty seconds, and that minute earth's contents recover moulting capability as well as faded anger with the presto of amoebean verses then walking forever instead of getting it back for nothing might turn the whiteout to remuda and you'd at least have hooves for tracks.

FOUR. Paratasein choice cut pickled and un knowing gravel to be one of the conditions of such motion slipp/ed from the pleasing though numbing eutaxia-tatooed sameness instead of.

FIVE. Is this an attempt to crack spin or a catalytic sugar made up to cotton the sweet uses of adversity with story's *then* planted in those spaces instead of poetry's timed gaze pivoted on possibility as opposed to prose's loss and what is measure pointing at if not that quaquaversal heat mountained up and spooned as dancing.

SIX. The sign of the turn plowed back into place as this world wheel scoops out preaction in a twinkle circumcizes heart such typhoon has no seersucker no milk no sugar.

SEVEN. If this renovation of memory turns out to be dérimage and we have to steer for the new world yet again in an elenxis of substitution then what now when the serial is only cinema and lists are needed before any action other than fishing which is best when it just *is* and not *for* anything.

EIGHT. Authority without text an illusion to master the distant and dissolving perimeter without search or government escaped containerism offers the tyranny of hot stuff contraband and never conquered without the fix or need for *dromenon* without the hook.

NINE. What drew river to share earth neither overtaking word was old scratch upon the world root radical that makes us taste like licorice unless you're white try ginger.

TEN. One reason why decimal was spotted on both sides of the centum/satam line was like the falling angel concurrently sighted with the same combination or polarity of surrender to the *hieros* except for the bird clouds interception of those tattooed letters rising from the city and maybe even this kind of patching of the rag.

ELEVEN. So there's this straight line to the question of hunger no way around the correct posturing of rule or guide me o righteousness not to answer but middle voice clot plugged with love-stutter simply wide need.

TWELVE. At first anguish squeezed news out of a hostile terminology for red yellow black and brown but pretty soon languages become mouths of painful non-tint jargon poking into the dream and then all of a sudden with snare-drum crackling that heave of gut and protest untumbles the lock and *kapow*!

THIRTEEN. Sans souci the tongue hunts description until each morpheme gains kinaesthesis and then sharp motion pictures the memorable rousing as smoke or at least poked colour when smoked red.

FOURTEEN. Scope out the paragrams ahead and see if the divine isn't inhabited by some once-upon-a-time intention negotiable by a *shh shh* creeping up on curiosity as a kind of campground lure or kick the can espionage chance-cast into the emic abacus crying alley alley home free or any other text-spect (in-spect, re-spect, ex-pect).

FIFTEEN. After a while opinion becomes fierce burning and no longer dream has itself straight on how far from the cedar home is nor could nothing come in pieces even though tainted such dexterity in the world tree's branches takes hold and all you can do is shake violently these little boxes for books.

SIXTEEN. At least precious peace and the Friday sapphire are still pupa'd into the sanctuary of message where anima equals the last bark of joy.

You want to know until I found you and your skin which sits in itself language was to me a system out there others thought up but I couldn't.

That story of the moon about her eye knocked out isn't what they told me.

You see, I don't remember any other than the sun and moon stuff or mountain mystery almost as "truculent fingerless chamaco" better to be the bird or owl of poetry so I could just do it by itself without being surrounded by these masters of the "arrow" I don't know the surface of unless "it" literally is techne art is the only environment this paper and all the touch brought to that skin I know the action I'm capable of'll only get done by blood as the life of the mind thought not so silent just thinking of God rather the log sun scooped out his boat from or the cedar Enki drummed with I know exactly every time story happens I have memory back.